THE SLEEPING BEAUTY

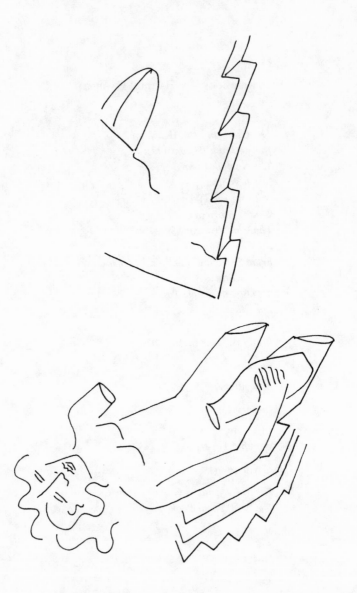

Susan Bush

THE
SLEEPING
BEAUTY

HAYDEN CARRUTH

HARPER & ROW, PUBLISHERS, New York
Cambridge, Philadelphia, San Francisco,
London, Mexico City, São Paulo, Sydney

1817

FIRST EDITION

Designer: Robin Malkin

Library of Congress Cataloging in Publication Data

Carruth, Hayden, 1921–
   The sleeping beauty.

   I Title.
PS3505.A77594S59   1982   811'.54   82-47518
                                                  AACR2
ISBN 0-06-015021-1   82 83 84 85 86 10 9 8 7 6 5 4 3 2 1
ISBN 0-06-090973-0 (pbk.)   82 83 84 85 86 10 9 8 7 6 5 4 3 2 1

DEDICATION

Acknowledgments

Many people, too many to be listed, heard or read this poem in its various stages of composition and offered useful criticisms. However, those whose help was crucial, in differing ways, to the completion of the work should not go unrecognized: Linda Arking, Susan Bush, Donald Hall, Galway Kinnell, Carolyn Kizer, James T. McCartin, Joanne Meschery, and Judith Weissman. Further thanks go to Susan and Bob Arnold of Green River for printing one section from this sequence in their *Longhouse;* to the John Simon Guggenheim Memorial Foundation and the National Endowment for the Arts for fellowships granted during the composition of the poem; and to Yaddo of Saratoga Springs where important parts of the poem were written during three separate residencies.

THE SLEEPING BEAUTY

1

Ich hab' mein' Sach' auf Nichts gestellt.
—*Johann Wolfgang von Goethe*

Out of nothing.

                This morning the world was gone;
Only grayness outside, so dense, so close
Against the window that it seemed no season,
No place, and no thought almost,
Except what preys at the edge of thought, unknown;
But it was snow. The flakes, extremely fine
And falling unseen, still made the bough
Of the hemlock whiten. Here and now—
Twig by twig, needle by needle—a plume
Reached through the grayness,
Intricate purity that somehow could assume
Its own being in its own space,
Out of nothing . . .
                or out of a cold November
Dawn that anyone could see, this grace
That no one can ever quite remember.

2

Then from beyond, from nowhere, from the wilderness,
As in a little dance stirring the hemlock plume,
Comes wind. And out of silence
Words gather.
                    Within the room
The inhabitant looks out, unknown, unseen,
A presence gathering.
                    So this pure loveliness
Of the moving air, unseen equally,
Is truly the world's breath, truly
The spirit, invisible and from nowhere,
                              though it moves
The hemlock's whitened branch
In slow swaying rhythms that are real and proves
For every beholding this actual dance,
This beauty, which is also love.
                              Alone
Consciousness gathers, a nothing, silence that chants
Unheard in the room, a poem made
                              slowly
                                    by no one.

3

As movement seen, so is the sound, the singing,
Heard; wherefore a tremulous hope has ever
Down dim centuries sought the joining
Of these two powers together
In efficacy, in the world, in concrete meaning—
Hope forlorn now, which can be no beginning,
For the word is silent, and the word within
The word is silent . . .
                    Oh, begin
In all and nothing then, the vision from a name,
This Rose Marie Dorn,
Woman alive exactly when the Red Army came
To that crook of the Oder where she was born,
Woman who fled and fled in her human duty
And bore her name, meaning Rose in the Thorn,
Her name, the mythologos, the Sleeping Beauty.

4

Three persons are here, of whom the first
Is *you*, dear princess, you who are always sleeping,
Thou therefore addressed—
Thou in thy quiet-keeping—
As if immutably; and yet you dream. You rest
And you dream this world. You are mystery. You exist.

Second is *he*, the prince. He lives
Wherever and whenever he perceives
Himself in your dreaming, though in fact he is awake
And so knows the horror of being
Only a dream.

Third is the poem, who must make
Presence from words, vision from seeing,
This no one that uniquely in sorrow rejoices
And can have no pronoun.

Last, as in all dreaming,
Is heard the echo of coincidental voices.

5

You then. Your eyes hooded, shrewd a little,
Feminine always.
                    Remember how you lay
Shadowed in your name, naked in your beauty,
Waiting? Could you say
For whom (as he came to you), or for what encounter?
Was it yes, no, despair or hope? Or nothing?
                                                Mortal
And eternal in mortality, Rose,
Named the Dornröschen, Princess
Of the Briar Rose, were you dreaming of *him*,
Our history?

            Holy
Breath of creating love and harmony and time,
O Spirit,
            she sleeps. How insecurely
Words try her momentous dreaming. Let the song
Sing, from that inward stress, this world so surely
Created in her sleep,
                    this beauty in its centuries of wrong.

6

Your dream:
        His name was Homer. He was blind.
He had *gone blind*—so your dream tells you. Sight
Of the human brutality of mind
Put out his eyes, a light
Drowned at the beginning, he then confined
To dimmest story, as to its powers resigned:
How once upon the wall of Priam's
City, between the swarming armies,
Walked (and you dream the dust on her bare feet)
A woman tossed up there
By breaking waves of men heaving in heat,
In rancorous, fecund, Asian air,
The fury of romance. Surging, resurging, wet
With blood and the seminal ooze, they broke that fair
Goddess and queen. Her name was Helen. Yet

7

Was she the innocent? Too beautiful for that,
Already in time's dawn too washed with the lurid
Sunstreakings of romance, she had caught
The coupling habit, torrid
Duplexities of love and death (or fact
And fancy, real and ideal); then she grew fat
And in her old age called out names
Of men that scorched her throat, the flames
Blind Homer saw. No, innocence was his
Whom Homer called not brave
But more than brave, who in the world that is
Knew himself victim, dead to save
The stupid heroic pride of the prime defector
In history, and still went out and gave
His life without hope or despair. His name was Hector.

8

Recurrently he also dreams:
                              A girl, seventeen, fair
Complexioned, black hair in a widow's peak,
Black eyes. French Canadian. Her bare
White slender body seeks
Him down the years, decades, with that bright flare
Of blood at her thighs, an emblem, and her stare
Is hooded but accusing; yet how
Can he make amends? He takes her, slow
And very gentle, joining himself to her wound
That he did not, could not, give,
Loving her completely so that no sound
Escapes him. Again and again to live
Only for her in his humility, her blood-flame
Burning him. Again and again her fugitive
Glance at him, hooded eyes always the same.

9

As Doctor Peter said:
                    "Dreams about a menstruating
Woman may often mean a castrated man,
Your need to dominate him. Screwing
The girl is your oedipal vanquishment
Of your father, his un-manning."

                              Shock. Undoing
The dream. Oh, not the father-maiming, crude
As it seemed, but rather the shattering
Of his dream-mood, all that mattered,
The loving and lovingkindness, the steadfastness
In existential sorrow,
The hard and human need to share—all blasted.
Could he accept it?
                    Sorrow, sorrow,
The deeper wound in loving.
                              That it was force,
Power, even in the giving, this was his sorrow.
He was man, *a* man, flawed in his very source.

10

Your dream:
> His name was Hero, and his other name
Was History
> emerging from the mists   your maker
Whom you made, your dream who came
With his sword for his scepter.

And from his right hand sprang understanding both of time
    and of fame
And his gorgeous brawn was only gentleness a peace in
    Cockayne
And in the cities of the mist, stone rising
On stone
> and the pennons flying.

The sword that was scepter changed to a pipe of song.

His name was Hero/ was History/   was He/
Ego in all its radiance come from a long
Distance across the unknown sea
Shining/

> for he carried death in his left hand death in his
    eyes
And from them fashioned love, both the look and the gift,
    compassionately.

And your dream made him.
> He was yours and he was wise.

11

Your dream:
                His name was Herod. No? How close
In the TV's little window he comes, smiling
Into your privacy, he with his nose
So uglily beguiling
Like a lover's. You know somehow this shows
His power, his personal sympathy. He avows
The national interest and your own safety
In this new administrative program, so weighty
A decision, and he sighs for the infants smothered
(Practically painless) to avert
"Our peril." Where did he come from? He has hovered
On the screen for years, the tie, the shirt
Always impeccable. Galatian? Greek? Jew?
Who knows? A politician. Some provincial upstart
Willing to do what nobody else would do.

12

"We thought the chateau was safe. The men were gone,
Of course, all except Uncle Hypolyte
Half dead with dropsy. *They* came in the dawn
And took us without a fight—
Naturally. And then they chose me. Roughly, 'Come on,'
They said, 'you're the prettiest.' Out over the lawn
In my bare feet in the cold dew,
Pushed, dragged, flung to the avenue
Of old beeches,

         where at the biggest I was bound.
And they spread my feet wide
And nailed them with whittled pegs to the ground
And built a slow fire of twigs inside
My skirts and fed it until I was aflame.
'Eh, damsel, how like you this for fucking?' one cried.
God, it was almost a kind of ecstasy when it came!"

13

Your dream:
         His name was Hesiod, a darkish man
Filled with goodness, both of the earth and the gods
(For in those days these two were one),
Who still was litigious and made
Lawsuits against his brother, and was murdered then—
For his goodness? The dream is inexplicit. Down
Rows of millet in a shining field
He walks, upward among the fig trees
Where someone with a club springs out. That's it.
He knew how far it was
(Being a poet) to Tartarus: the distance a brazen bit,
Falling below ground, would traverse
Equal to the fall from sun to earth. And so he fell.
He left you works and days, gods of the universe,
And was murdered, and you wept, and he went to hell.

14

Your dream:
>   His name was Hannibal, *i.e.*, by Baal's
Grace. Baal, god of locality. And on Alpine ridges
Where Baal dwelt he marched his incredible
Elephants, and down the edges
Of Italia fighting, yet loved by many, by all
The ordinary people, for justice, so that Africa
Might have come to Europe, new
Light in the dark of Roman law,
Nor for justice alone but leniency, the human idea;
Yet Rome prevailed
And has always prevailed, and drove him to Syria,
Crete, Bythnia, always exiled,
Always!
>   Wandering grace of the native god,
Place to place passing, lost light in the field
At night, candle in history, moving toward your bed.

15

Called him "Big Joe" yes and Joe Turner it was his name
And he sang yes he sang
                     well them deep down country blues
With a jump-steady and a K.C. beat   that came
From his big old heart and his bouncing shoes
From that big old bouncing voice

  Baby, you so beautiful and you gotta die someday

                           the same
As those Kansas City nights   huge boozy flame
Of the miserloos and the careless joys/   But slow
He could sing it too when it took him   sorrow
In the bone   slow

    Broken the ten commanmint,
    Beat out with the jinx,
    Can't sometimes
    Get water to drink,
    Ain't got a mount to jack in,
    Can't produce a dime,
    I'm jus as raggdy
    As a jay-bird in whistlin ti—
                   ime____

                       over and over

In the gathering of souls the flickering
Of human destiny that sways to discover
Happiness in fate.   And it was music, music.
"Shouter," they called him. And great is what he was,
Warm and   reckless   and accurate and   big—

Saint Harmonie,
       touch thou these lines with Turner's voice.

16

There where pines darken the water above the brookbed
Rita beckoned, pointing down to a woman's face
She had put there, "Because," she said,
"This is a secret place
And one cares for disposing of what one's made,
Even the failures." In half-relief the head
Looks upward through rippling water,
Askance, half turned back, caught
As if by its origin in the earth again.
There, beneath the waterflow
And changing reflections, pine trees, sun, and rain,
A face, although people come and go
And Rita has gone and the secret is all that stays,
As the presences of the poem alone can know,
A woman's face looks up from the water, always.

Oaks and dark pines, remote, the northern forest.
What does the woman's face in the water mean?
Traces of snow. This the oldest, the purest,
Naiad alive in the stream,
Ophelia drowned in eternity. She nearest
And most distant, coldest, stillest, dearest.
Crystals gleam in the brown leaves
Without sunlight. Mythological lives
Exist in dreams. Leaves twist and turn in the current,
Drift over the face and on.
Passage and change obscuring the eternal moment.
The feminine in a face of stone
Unchanged, there in cold water, the face of sleep.
Wind in the pines. Dream sound. Snow. Alone.
Woman. Forever. Water. Watching. Deep.

18

" 'Thee knows. Must thee not knowe?' I so saying
Evere & againe, but onely within my Minde,
Whenso he Snorreth, after his *Plaieing*
That him so gratifieth;
Then creppit I to Candel, softlie, praying
(Mine *Blasphemie!*) the Quille not scritch, bewraying
Mine Hande in th' Colde; I tho't Godd
Griev'd not of my Scriving. What!
Cou'd I not helpe mee? No. 'Twas him I feart,
A Manne, wou'd hee not see
Oure Candel shorten'd? Once hee upsterted
From Sleepe & lookt wide-eied at mee,
But seeth not. Mine owne pretties, on his olde Sermons
Wrot twixt the lines—now fownd! 'Mistris, be thee
Simple?' & hee laied them, babes, to th' fier burning."

19

He said:
        All right then, I *was*, o.k.? Screwing
My father. Sticking it to him for all he'd done.
I know it. Can I refuse
To know? Dominion
Is sweet, revenge sweeter, and who's
To say either or both couldn't produce
A dream's gratifications? Let
Pleasure defend itself. And yet . . .

What I remember is still so very much more
Than pleasure, or even
Than love's gravest working, for it was my pure
Concern. The given
Was her hurt and her womanly sense of wrong.
What I gave was what can never be proven,
Myself, nothing, to be used by her, to belong

To her, to *be* her, that her hurt and wrong be mine.
It was love, yes, but love rarified, burned
In the crucible. And so it has always been.
Has it? To be concerned,
What does that mean—only pity? And then
What's pity if not only dominion
In another style?

        O Spirit,
Spirit of love inhabiting
Dark places of cities and bright places
Of the countryside, what
Is human meaning, what are those faces
Turned to one another? Is not
His loving more than the mere energy it seems,
A struggle to prove himself? He had thought
He could help you,
             wounded girl of his dreams.

21

Spirit
> let there be even in the last hour
Even in the scorching of the air
> > > a song of love/
Spirit
> this is their only power
All that they can perceive
Of their human being   their only invention   the
> flower
Of consciousness/

> [Brother Estlin, he misjudg'd thee & thou'rt
Unforgiving.]

> > What they have made
Is this invisible   in the void
Of visibilities, of animal vacancy
> > > the bones
That snarl the stars that gnash
The trees in their imperturbable march like lions
Home from the kill/
> > Out of the wash
Of the tides of essence licking their wet souls
Wearing them away
> > > they made this
> > > > hush
Of existence
> love perdurant
> > > harmony
> as of the flight of many gulls.

22

Your dream:
        His name was Hölderlin. Ah, name, name!
Syllables gliding in Teutonic rhapsody
From classic order to the sweet insane,
As he in his *Abendphantasie*
Soared, his soul among rosy clouds. When the flame
Of heaven faded, when in eloquent twilight he came
Back to the garden, to you, the best
Was that darkening—ach, an Weltschmerz
Leidend, the tenderest passion. He knew that gothic tower
Deep in a forest standing,
So beautiful, so old, created in mind's power
To outlast the mind. And he knew heartrending,
The gravest and purest of loving. Beauty was worth
Its every sorrow, mind's fading or world's ending,
As darkness covered the garden that is the earth.

"Good-bye," they always whisper, "oh God," clinging—
And he walks down the steps in early lilac light
And she drives off in her Volkswagen
Into the snow-curtained street
And he turns and raises his hand by the elevator
And she clings sobbing and desperate at the stone gate
And he looks back in the autumn haze
From a distance under the yellow trees
And she finds his dear stinking pipe left on the bookcase
And he writes a letter
Ten pages long and tears it up and mails a postcard
And "Good-bye."
                "Good-bye."
                        "Good-bye."
                                Never
Shall they meet again.

                        Good-bye whispered, murmured,
                                            furled
In the creative wind,
                incredible cosmic command
                                to sever,
Disjoin, separate, break—
                death in the world.

24

You are the dreamer who dreams the world, and yet,
Princess, the world dreams you. There is never
A beginning. You create and are created,
Legend forever,
The lore of all human being, the victim who begets
Victimization; and your heroes, those who wait
For your invention, love and destroy you
As you will, you who can have no will—
Naked, spelled, fixed in the storm and flood
Of civilization, the bound
Of thorny fire, the wall of the bloom of blood.
You are known and you are never found.

Spirit, she is the vortex. Placidly she sleeps
While the heroes run impeccably round and round
About their business. Only the poem weeps.

25

He thinks how often when his semen spews
It feels like blood. A hot leakage, burning.
How awkward! He remembers the Hindus—
Do not they wake in mourning
Invariably, their seed unrenewable? They choose
Each night between loving and dying. Then she—does
It burn her, too? Are we joined,
Victim-lovers, everyone, in this wound
Of fire forever? Do all men feel their lives
Taken in the heart of love?
Does it mean something? Anything?

                      Thus he contrives
Enigmas from horror. He would prove
That the simplest human realities unfold
Mysteriously, and that in this knowledge he may move
Without change. Yet daily he sees himself grow old.

26

You lay there then on that couch as if in effigy
(How do women get out of their clothes so fast?)
Or as if an emblem, not at all stiff,
But quiet, luminous, composed,
Or so it seemed to him, your arms by your sides,
Legs straight, hair flowing around your face,
Your eyes lidded and your lips
Formed in the merest smile, nipples
Erect. The cloth beneath you, heavy brocade
Of shaded purple and gray,
Might have been stone. He looked. Were you awaiting
A transfiguring or a violation?
You did not, you probably could not, say. The moment
Was its momentum.
      Was this then why you lay
So still? He trembled, touched near his own torment.

27

Wind in the pines, a dark, damp, Novemb'ring wind,
And here with small, small song the redpolls flittering,
Branch to branch, maybe nine of a kind,
And here an oak leaf skittering
Down the cold brook, in its brown curl holding nine
Grains of new snow, maybe you and your almost divine
Eight sisters quarreling to your lover,
Cold Orpheus, where he waits; and over
The brook maybe your small, small souls flit on
Cheeping their quarreling song
Per una selva oscura, downstream and down
The humid wind, your boat sailing along,
A curled brown leaf of oak, nine new grains of snow,
Past the stone face of the lady of water, sung
Through these dark woods by nine little birds as they go.

Why dost thou tear me? Had I done thee hurt?
For my name you took me
            which was Lilith.
                           Cunt
Was my name, the sweet thing wild & furtive
On the grass plain and the mountain.
Woman was my name.
                  Perché mi scerpi?
With the moon I was
          and the lion
                  and you tore me,
You uprooted me in your lust
Of enviousness and you beat down my breast
As you beat down unripe fruit from the olive bough,
You made my womb broken
And I walked in pain.
               Lilith I was. Now
I am the pain-walker, the all-taken,
But Lilith I was. I was.
                Perché mi scerpi?
There
      only my cry is left
        like wind in the bracken.
Here
      I am death. You made me. Now
        why do you tear me?

29

Late. The back road "slicker than owl shit." Snow
Packed hard under new powder. No tracks;
No one has been this way. Then the doe
Leaps into the headlights, a fixed
Snow-dripping instant. The truck fishtails, slews,
Spins, a great rounding out of control
And over the left bank, Jesus, backward
Into the ravine; a crunch, a lurch.
Five thousand pounds of metal too heavy to crush.
Almost slow; a wrenching.
Silence. Lights out. Damage. Disgust. Push
The door upward, its weight in this dimension
Unknown before. The doe had been small; her hoofmark
Will trail to gnawed fur this winter. Slip out, clenching
For the drop. Groan. Crawl upward through the dark.

Upward through the dark, this . . .
                                        this non-entity
Moving from the objective crash in pained ascension
To surpass the disaster of identity,
To seek the greater intention,
Greater energy, greater coherence, a supra-entity
In a free existence, the completed person in personality,
Out from the bondage of blood and nerves,
Beyond history, between the stars,
Pure subjectivity in its spirit, its spiritual
Outreaching and inreaching,
For which no ceremony of love, no ritual,
No convention, and no teaching
Can suffice, but only love transcendent in the wreck
Of the determinant world, love continually searching
Beyond love,
        the poem crawling upward through the dark.

31

Your dream:
         His name was Hermann, tender, quiet,
Suffering, he who in his dream dreams you,
Dreaming. All fuses. Your eternal night
Is alive with stars, with moons,
With moving lanterns, shapes of Walpurgis light
Elegantly frightening, terrifying. And yet
Strains of harp-playing, Mozartiana,
And words, half-heard, of far hieratic
Resonances fill your fear with love,
Shy love by a northern
Expanse of water where the sea eagles rove
On strange incongruous winds. Thorns
Darken your dreaming. He is Hesse, he is mystery,
Steady and blue, lover, die Polare, der Nordstern.
All confuses. Death & love. Music & cruel story.

Blizzard in the mountains. Dusk. The cabin's light
Pales in these sheets of snow flung peak to peak,
Crag to crag, the essential might
Of everything. What's one weak
Lamp?
      A paradox. That in a wild night
Self alone through self to self can sight
Ego's perilous voyage, to sustain
Freedom and being finally in the dawn
Beyond ego.
      So the great determinant winds,
Mindlessness of the universe,
Wrack the cabin, and the boards crack and the mind's
Timber with them. Worse, it is always worse,
It is never better.

      Ahi! Who art thou, *lo buon*
Maestro? And hast thou forever gone?

      What course
Shall the voyager plot now, unguided, alone?

The point is (maybe) that the woman's face was *made*.
Rita made it. Then because it was (she said)
Flawed, she placed it in the brook, *conveyed*
It there, the woman's head
Looking up forever (almost), serene and sad.
Out of earth it came, in Rita's hands created,
In Rita's ecstasy: *out of herself*
She made it. Thus it is thought and feeling—
A meaning. And if none of us can say quite what
It is and none can say quite all,
Still it is there, our meaning mystery in the water,
Our eternity, both less and more than awful
Timelessness and nothing. It is what we make of them,
Our mythic soul (dear Rita's) against the flowing
Water, which really is forever and mind-forsaken.

34

The poem moves north.
                    "Good-bye."
                              "Good-bye."
                                        North
In dark dawn to Vermont, snowflakes drifting
Among the pines, a pickup, a Ford
¾-ton, F-250,
4-wheel-drive, rusty green with one door
Crimped shut forever and a busted gear
Banging in the front axle.
                    "Good-bye."
(O God, clinging.)
                    North is the way,
Bearing this image, Susan, the slight girl
Beneath great trees
Standing half-turned, head bowed, a swirl
Of yellow hair.
          "Good-bye."
                    The windshield
Fogs in the cold and the snowfall thickens. North
Is the way, and loneliness, the snow-blurred field,
Existence, seeking what a life is worth,

In the exigencies of consciousness,
Of language,—the poem moving.
                                    In Argyle
Out front of the American Legion post
Is an old ten-pounder with a pile
Of cannonballs, the usual pyramid, but cased
In metal strapping bolted to a concrete base
So no one can steal them.
                                    Remember
When people didn't steal things?
                                    Damned
If I do. But anyway I mind when they didn't
Bother with nothing small.
Railroads more likely.
                          Who's that?
                                    They wan't hidden
Neither.
                  But who is that talking?
                                    Hell,
I seen when they hijacked the will of the people
                                    —Who? Who?—
Like it wan't no more than a barrel of spruce oil.
You know it same as I do. Call me Amos.
                                    You?

You, Amos? But you're dead now.

There's a many

Will say so.

You burned out in that schoolbus

You were living in, up on Stannard Mountain.
The warden told us.

Cuss

The warden.

But he found your body.

Maybe. Maybe

It were a doe I had, for eating purposes. But mainly
In my condition you can't hardly tell
What's fact and what's a story.

Well,

What is your condition?

Nobody knows.

Nobody?

You. And you always said
You ain't nobody. Correct me if I'm wrong.

O.K.,

But you must be somewhere.

Dead. All dead,

Me and mine. Or just for the hell of it let's say
I got me a little trailer now, a place to hide,
The upper side of Bear Swamp off Wolcott way

Back of Budbill's where it dreens offn the ledges. Snugger
Than a cat's ass in them balsams there. You won't
Locate it easy, no sir.
                                        The truck
Slows, slips into the slant
Of a roadside turn-off. Silence and the shock
Of stopped motion. Nothing moves. Except . . .
                                                    Look

There, twenty feet off, that dead elm
With the broken branch. See that owl?
A great horner too, sitting so still the snow
Has draped him. Only
His yellow eyes, blinking once, give him away
In the soft gray snowscape.
                            Hungry
Cuss, ain't he? Hunting by daylight. Blind
As a cow in a barnfire. Have to be mighty lucky
To catch a meal that way, seem's-zo. I mind

When them old hooters had plenty eating material
Round these parts, and other folk too. Course
That were times gone. You could prevail
With but fourteen head of cows
Then, if you had the makings.
                                        Makings?
                                                What I call
Makings of a man. And that means straight out all
The time, with childern on the way,
A orchard, garding, a fair stand of hay,
Pigs, chickens, you know—what we meant by farming
In those days. It's all changed now.

Last night's empties spill from a broken carton
Still glittering under thin snow
Where there's a faint yellow pattern, somebody's name
Written in urine.
                        Northward now.
                                        Past old houses,
Farms fallen, or some still working, pride and shame

Mingled in windows stuffed with grainsacks, "Lots
For Sale" nailed to the dooryard maple. Or past
Rich men's farms, "shelters," only not
For them, more for their taxes—
Painted houses, barns upright, then the paddocks
With matched Belgians bred for show, too big to work,
Too feisty to handle, pawing the snowy
Turf with elephantine hooves.
                                        Amos,
You there?
            Where?
                        Anywhere where you can hear.
Listen. In a pine forest
Downcountry, in a secret place, not far, in a clear
Smooth-running brook, there's a face. It's
A woman, Amos. Always there, always looking
Up through the water.
                        I know. Goddamn it, yes,
I knowed afore you was thought of—her lurking

40

Down there like. Maybe not the same, of course.
But I seen her, God's truth, and more than once.
Even in Big Bear Swamp where the water's
Blacker than the innards of a crankcase
I saw her, by Jesus, so I backpaddled like crazy,
And when those ripples cleared off there she was,
Down in the watergrass, just as plain, as calm—
Like she was laying out somewhere in the rowan
At blackberrying time.

Who is she, Amos?
Come on,
Who do you think, for Christ's sake!
Who do you think, Amos?
Hell, a woman,
The woman—that's all.
Asleep or awake,
Amos?
Both.
Who knows her, Amos?
Them that come
Where I come from.
In all this does she make
Any difference, Amos?
Yes. I reckon. Some.

He reads there, only a boy, fifteen, in the dingy
Corner of the library where he has found these books,
The forgotten ones, perhaps the forbidden,
Bakunin and Johann Most,
Emma Goldman and that dearest of all princes,
Piotr Kropotkin. He reads as he has not since,
Engrossed. And then he walks out in the night,
Going where warm house-lights
Gleam in repeated patterns across the mist
And rain; dismayed, in wonder
Of these rich houses. And like a somnambulist
He walks in a trance of compassion. Under
The dripping trees he pauses, he dreams of pain,
Pain everywhere, pain forever, the cosmogonal blunder,
And his little tears fall down in the great rain.

42

"For fifteen years he never knew I never
Came. The jerk. I faked, but anyone could have told.
At last, 'Maybe it could be better,'
I said. 'Why don't we go
To one of those counselors?' and we did. Then after
A spell we stopped. That was in '65. It's later
Now. It's goddamn '75, and two years ago
He 'came out,' as he called it, he went gay,
And I'm—so soon, would you believe it?—I'm in
   menopause,
And I don't feel so good,
And no matter what, the diet, the exercise,
I don't age nicely. Too much droop—
Chin, breast, belly, ass. He said I should forget.
And I said what the hell's the use. I sit on this stoop
In this same old chair where grandmother used to set."

His dream:
>He is dressed in a white sheet, riding
Hellbent on a bicycle down a straight white road
Between snowbanks brilliantly high and wide,
And his belly is brilliantly broad.
And the hospital, when at last it comes in sight,
Is a disused railway station, empty inside
And cold; but the birth is easy, a mere gush
Or a happy purging, and behold! in the flash
Of newborn radiance is a beautiful translucent child
With huge eyes like sapphires
And hair of streaming yellow flame; and he is wild
With joy, joy, joy, the stars
On the ceiling are shining and chiming like bells,
The snow is dancing, the trees a triumphal chorus,
Because he has done it at last,
>the real thing,
>>he has done it himself!

44

Your dream:
               His name was Hilarity but he never laughed,
Your average mimic, your stumblebum storyteller,
Poet, etc., "well acquainted with death,"
Th' apparition i' th' mirror,
On whom alone he smiled; his ally, his grotesque.
Who else had taught him all his comic craft—
Despair and terror? So with bedpan irony
He made bones out of chestnuts. Sly?
God, they broke up, holding their sides in horror,
Gagging, the mirthful mortals!
His asides were held the gallstones of his era.
Famous he was. More than that, exalted,
The top banana, honored for his Sisyphean demeanor
And after-dinner epitaphs. He upsets you, no? Yet all told
He may be your dream's key figure, the anti-dreamer.

45

Death, he thinks. In fact he has thought it every day
For fifty years, and every night, though someone had told
    him
It would grow easier. But no.
                      No.
                            Will they
Come then to help him, hold him,
All nine as he has always known them, to play
At last in that ending now not far away,
Together as he has always believed them,
The company of love in a final cohesion,
A final rapture? For concord was his assumption
Always. But no.
              No,
They will not come. His dream of the company
Of love, of its benevolence and openness
And lovingkindness and freedom, *freedom*, is only
A dream. They will not come, they will not come.
And he will die, like everyone, stupid and alone.

Wind sighing, crying, singing in the pines. Who knows
How to interpret the song? The snow falls
Thick or fine, altering the forms
Of land-imagery but clarifying
In water, this moving crystal above the charmed
Obsessive image. A woman's face looks upward
Always; in drapery now, for ripples
And swirls of sand have silted a little
Against her, and a few oak leaves have collected
For her décolletage.
She is half-taken by nature, she is half-accepted.
And so, half-turned to her shoulder, she gazes
Always upward, forbearant, unchanging. Memory
Knows her. In all her repetitions, image on image,
She gazes from time beyond time, from poems
                                    deep in the poem.

Half-turned, as if reluctant, the lady of water
Looks upward always, yet with gaze averted,
Gentle, unadmonishing, but grave, caught
In the changing but still eternal
Flow of crystal, between air and earth, thought
And intuition, but caught *there*, the margin unsought
But secret, not one sphere or the other;
There and also most distant, farther
From this than Isis or Inanna, and yet clear,
Or almost but not completely
Clear, in the reflecting crystal, the lady here,
Lady of paradox, drowned and alive, obliquely
Staring from darkness into the world of light,
Held in the crystal, held there proudly and meekly,
Staring, there always,
                              even in the dead of night.

Dornröschen, princess
    are not you too   held
In the crystalline moment of time stopped,
    you lying
So demurely propped,   naked and spelled,
On the couch of stone/
                The purifying
Of icy fire surrounds you/
                   Beyond it, quelled
Forever, is what might have been, for you,
    though the unimpelled,
Are the dreamer whose significant dreaming
Still brings,   dream by dream,   the seeming
That will be the world/
                You lie in the center,
The integration
And the nowhereness of all things,
    as seasons of being are separated
    by a winter/
O northern princess,
               see these apparitions,
How they gather in dreams, our history from the mist,
The meaningless, mysterious images of your dreaming
    reason
That you will know
           the instant you are really kissed.

49

You know what?
                    What, Amos?
                              It's Christly strange—
The way we are, I mean. Not like the animals.
I mind one time down to the Grange
Sucking up them venison meatballs
They put on at their annual supper to raise some change,
I seen Yewklid Morrison. Yewk had the mange
And a rumbling gut. He made me think
Of my old tom after that drink
Of monkeyjuice Luther Parkhurst give him. Hell,
We're all animals deep down,
I reckon. Yet not exactly. I could tell
Yewk was considering, I see him frown,
But I couldn't tell what. And then all those others,
Suddenly they seemed like they came from out of town,
Strangers, though they was my neighbors. Some
        was my own brothers.

Ain't that something? Why, I knowed old Tom,
Most as if I was a cat myself,
But not those people. And by God, I'm
People, right? Don't laugh;
To me it's something mighty close to crime.
There ain't none of us real.
                              Once I come
Down through the old graveyard on Clay Hill
In March in a snowstorm, and I heard a wail
Like all those stones was crying out their names;
And I could hear each one,
Davis and Dodge and Butler, Stearns and James,
And they was all of us, dead bone
Or beating heart, no difference, each a spook,
You, me, or Nigger Jim, and then that stone
You call the woman back there in that brook.

51

Your dream:

        His name was Hegel, a dear sweet man;
Nay, tho' 'a cou'dst na gabble it straitly, yet he saw
Straightway to the end of the brave Tristan
And the beautiful Iseult,
How they must die, oh, most needfully die, their own
Hands upon it—for sake o' th' higher synthesis. None
Saw it keenlier, none the entire
Realpolitik, how Romance doth aspire
(From those souls bound and dying) to life in the mass,
Freedom in history,
Being in cosmos. Oh, 'a was a darlin' man. Don't ask,
Dear dreamer, for the posterior story
Of life, freedom, and being, or where those bones do lie—
Tristan and Iseult and all. 'Twere mankind's glory,
And thine,
      and in thy dreaming hit mought make thee cry.

Named she was a Smith, born Smith, but how related
To any Smith on earth?—and she was called Bessie
And papa her beauty wan't very much in her face
Nor body neither she wan't nobody's baby
But she was just the most beautifullest known lady
Cause lord what she was was Woman yes and Grace
And well Sex papa and all them things twice
Over and more in that dark oh that powerful voice

Ain't no high yallah I'm a dee-ep chicken brown

And papa she meant it
For herself and all her people and women
And the human soul yes that's feminine that's musical
And there was a accident lord it was the end of song
Cause Clarksville they shut her out the honky hospital

Oh I'm a young woman   singing
            no it won't never end
                        and I ain't done nothing wrong.

53

He reads:
    "That is one of the great tragedies
Of revolutions: you have to suppress man
In order to save him."
                    But o Fidel,
"Suppress" means the camps,
It means "up against the wall," and good Cardenal
Who loves you and your revolution, the equalities,
The courage, the beautiful new nation,
Cardenal *saw* the camps, saw the oppression,
Cardenal saw the *State* . . .

                    He reads. He writhes.
He's old almost, he is
Fifty-five, yet still the boy-anarchist. These deaths
Are unbearable. No one is guilty
Enough for that (or everyone is). They say: choose.
But Spirit, he cannot, he can't. Then what shall he
Do?
    Nothing.
            He'll be. And he'll sing the blues.

As Rousseau was another, singing.
Everywhere man
Is born free, and everywhere
he is in chains.
Through history, as if in history's plan,
They rise, they flare like grains
Of meteoric fire, the great romancers, one
Following another, burning, burning.
Men
Must be forced to be free.
And passion
In romance must be love in action,
Lust for the ideal . . . oh, murderous . . .

All you great,
All you good and terrible
Straining forever in beauty and man's fate,
You heroes valorous in error,
Why could you not have let love be? And why
Was loving never enough?

Sing, Robespierre,
Of how your loves look, trundling past to die.

55

"Shock? Is that what you're asking? My dear, I was a
country girl, like you, like most of us, you understand?
What didn't we understand—about that! And it's all in the
texts anyway; and yes, there are those who read. You
yourself will learn. Besides,
 It was common knowledge. The seraglio has walls and
the walls have chinks. The real shock—though granted, I
knew it already—was how
 And in what degrees I was expected to conduct myself.
I had not, could not have, altogether anticipated the effect
of that. The bride
 Will smile just so, and just so much, and will bow
 Just here, kneel just there, prostrate herself at just such-
and-such an intimation. Exactness is all. You'll see. It is
called the Formulary of Submissiveness,
 Which was without doubt the worst of the instruction,
at least for me. The rest was easy, though I must say
explicit.
 Demonstrations with ivory facsimiles, done in
extraordinary detail. When, where, how to touch,
 And with what, et cetera. You are smiling? I was told
to crouch
 But not to spring, that was the essence. And all in
God's will, of course, and the doing it in His praise. So I did
my best.
 Still I confess I never to this day have understood
 Why virgins should be the particular gratification of a
lord's lust. Something's peculiar there. You'd think the
contrary, wouldn't you, in spite of the pre-bridal training?

But you are smiling again. You feel differently? You are thinking perhaps of *your* lust, *our* lust?

Well, as to that, my dear, what is it but service to our lord, and to such a lord? It is called *love;* remember that. A very magnificent lord, no? This is our election. This is what I was told.

A simulated ecstasy, if practiced to perfection, is better than actuality. The actual, if unavoidable, is to be strictly controlled. And so on. Not that I was ever the favorite,

Nor even second or third. And now I am somewhat old.

Reckon the time yourself if you can: age twelve to forty-two. Thirty years I've waited for death. And I suppose 'in the nature of things'—oh, patience of impatience!—there may still be another thirty to wait."

O.K., Fulke Greville: "None can well behold
With eyes/ But what underneath him lies." You,
Old Yankee progenitor for sure, old
Pragmatist. Yet construe
These that the poem sees, these hot and cold
On the pillow. Such a diversity. The bold
Wet laughter of Grisette, the strained
Nymphomaniacal graduate trained
On pleasure's last least itch, the placid smile
Of true deepgoing rapture,
The cool one coming for friendship's sake, the guile
Or the crude and crazy stare of the capture
That terror makes on ecstasy's last brink—
Union in love, Fulke Greville? Or union's fracture
As back into Selfhood's mystery all loves sink?

Then rapture is self in itself entranced. And love?
It comes in the understanding that may mean
Not taking, not giving, but just to live—

You see that light on the mountain,
Small in the remoteness of blue snow? Viola
Lives there with her man who is 25 years older
Than she is. And every week
When Viola comes to town, she looks—
Bodily radiance shining in her dark eyes—
At the flatlanders who ask
How she can stand it up there with that old guy.
Do they think Viola wears a mask?

Beyond rapture is freedom, somewhere far above
Or far below, where the self is newly unentranced.
Viola knows. She fucks with an old man,
        Free, living, and without age,
                and in many ways
                        and at any moment
                                they make love.

Your dream:
        His name is Heraclitus, and he is huge,
Kosmikos, the primeval mentality,
                his skin
Glowing and changeable and many-hued,
Earthen
    or a pelt of rosmarine
Flaming in aurora.
        And he bends over you as if in
    brooding,
A magnetic cloud,
        and he touches your breast,
               and your
    blood
Rouses in a thickened heat never felt
Until now,
      and his mouth burns on your feet,
Your thighs, your belly, your tongue, your eyes,
              he mounts
Over you and your vagina
Pulses and widens,
       your brain is a tightness, an agony
Of incredulity and eagerness.
          And your raging
Body is broken and shaken in the slow everlasting burst
Of mystery,

                    the atomic profusion, the galactic
                                            fires, winds, oceans,
            and you are
Molten,   undulant,
        conceiving
                    the whole idea of the universe.

59

Jays shrieking in the fir clump, a world enraged.
Blue figures hopping in snow-burdened boughs.
What for, Amos?
                    Them critturs! Always
Fussing, ain't they?—not like you
Or me.
            Zoön politikon?
                              Eyuh. If they ain't got cause
For hollering, they'll make one. But likely they has,
Now, by the sound of it.
                          Three bounds
In deep snow and the cat pauses, looking around
And up, forepaw in a curl and her eyes
Triangular with indignation.
The jays dive-bomb her, the shrieking intensifies,
She cowers.
            See? All that hell-raising
For a yellow kitty. And she wan't jay-hunting. Twelve
Below and she's hungry, just trying for a mouse-nest.
Them jays, they ought to be ashamed of theirself.

He goes out with his chainsaw into the cold bright
Winter morning, into the forest. The cabin
Needs fuel, it always needs fuel. The night
Has dropped snow, eleven
Inches gauged on the brown ash, a sagging weight
On his snowshoes. And he sings,
                                    My gal's gotta light
Like a lighthouse out to sea.
                                    And oh,
You loves, say,
                    do you feel him bestow
Loving on you, which is a valuing? It is your beauty
Given to you in his seeing,
Your intelligence in his thought, so that truly
You become, you are becoming, in his being,
As he in yours. For loving is how you create
Each other, all of you, bestowing and believing
Together.
            Well, my gal's gotta light like a light-

House out to sea.
                    And he has dropped a dead gray birch
In the snow and is limbing it when his left snowshoe
Slips. Snarling, the saw leaps; he lurches;
The chain snags his bootlace—
And the motor stalls. Gasp. He looks at his unsevered
Foot, in astonishment. Alone, completely, in the forest.
(So many tone-rows. Spirit, will
They ever come together?)
                    You call,
One by one, lovers, through the distances: He's alive!
Alive!
        He yanks the lanyard
And begins bucking the birch for his Glenwood stove.
Alive. Somehow it is important,
Not because he matters, himself there like a tree
Among other trees, but because you have accorded it.

And ever time she smile she shine her light on me.

Your dream:
        His name was Hermes, and he was all to all,
The thief loved by peasants, who thus made him their
    boundary
Keeper and took him friendlily for their god
Of place and property;
Yet he was a great musician. He rejected the old
Conservatory music and sang the blues in a mode
Anyone could respond to. So they wanted him
Close by them always; he was psychopompos
Conducting their dead souls to hell, and he was herm,
Their phallus in the garden,
Guardian of the bed.
        He is guardian of your dream,
Dear sleeper,
        uniter of commerce and art,
Possession and beauty. His cleverness permits your world,
For he is your holy hermetic hoodlum, your secret.
Yet he told it all to Dionysus, your dreadful child.

Your dream:
        His name was Husband, his title Herr,
Noblest denomination, since he came from God
In the olden tongue. So he was tiller of your
Sweet soil, as of your close abode
Defender, and his rod was magical. Given to war
It was the outthrusting blade, or in your fire
The gentle stoker. And at times he rode a horse,
Going before you, and at times a hearse,
Leading the way to heaven.
                  But first and always
He was Herr Husband,
Householder, Handyman to all your joys,
And if he stumbled or looked askance
You had only to think your clever sexual thought
That brought him to his parfit gentillesse again,
Your knightly teacher whom none but you had taught.

The full of the moon. In pine woods a snowlight
Shines under the trees everywhere and is shadowless.
It were as if an earthlight, bright
Only by day's absence,
Arose, mysteriously radiant, in the night—
"But reflection, it is all reflection." High and white,
The moon looks down on her sister,
Who gazes back, askance, eastward,
Alone in the water. This is a spectral instance,
Light as it is in dreaming,
Its twice angled remoteness a transcendence
Or an alluding sourcelessness, a seeming,
Which only mythological sisters may embody
In this world. Cycle and stasis. Gleaming
And obscure. These two, together and solitary.

65

Odds & ends:
                    Enosburg Falls & Geof's cabin,
The lamplight, a fir bough scratching the eaves,
Snow kicking the windows. Geof croons
To his Mexican jumping bean,
"Hey friend, little worm, come out—don't you long
To come out?" Answer: "He's probably wondering
Why in God's name you don't come in."
And Janet laughed & laughed, and everyone
Had another slug of Geof's reefer.
                                        Postscriptum
In medias . . .
                    And meanwhile
Margery weeps. The first year, aphasic, bedridden,
Paralyzed—still her courage held;
But now the second. "She cries a lot." Hey friend,
Little Spirit,
                hast thou any power?

                                        Delirium,
This talk of art & love, the odds & the ends!

66

He remembers:
                 There was this big house they called the
   Hatch,
Or sometimes the Laughing Academy, which had barred
   grilles
On its windows, for every door a latch
And an appropriate lock called Yale
That was big and brassy with a key in someone else's
   possession,
And inside there he suffered interrogation, torture
When they wired his head to voltage and shocked him
Deep into the abyss, so that when he woke
He couldn't remember who he had been, and they did it
Again and again, and he sighed,
"Why? What have I done?" and usually they evaded
The question, but sometimes they said,
"Nothing, son, nothing at all—you're just unlucky,"
And he stood by the window in a dirty draft of cold,
Looking out, and he saw benches and sidewalks

Rise up and proclaim themselves, and his skin
Crawled on his body, a tear strolled down his nose,
And months later they said again,
"You're jinxed, son, you'll always
Be this way," and he saw his life sink down
In a melted gray heaving mass like a broken brain,
The chairs ignored him, the calendar
On the wall masturbated shamelessly, relentlessly,
Until years later they said, "O.K., you can go now,
Everything has been done,"
And he stepped to the door, but then he did not know how,
And he turned as if he had lost someone,
And they threw him out, and "Why?" he still whispered,
    "Why?"
Knowing no answer would come to him under the sun
Or anywhere else, whether he should live or die.

Your dream:
          His name was Hendryk Hudson. And oh,
    the glory!
Sailing so splendidly up that lordly river,
White canvas arching!
               Could any story
From the time before forever
Ever be more entrancing?
                  Yes, that was very
Nearly what it was, sunlight so merry
On the wavelets, white clouds mirroring
Those brave sails.
              Such a northfaring!
And such a land, this land, the *new found land*,
    hills
Greening on every side,
Appearing all as if from beyond time,
                   and all
For you, dear sleeping princess.

                Hide,
O Spirit—can you?—her dream from the blood those shores
Will come to. Can you?

             How beautiful! What pride—
The little *Half Moon*, sailing her *tour-de-force!*

Shall he then finally "put away childish things,"
Cunts, cocks, and similar ornaments, being
Grown old? So crude, so sudden. He sings
The blues in a broken singing
Now, impotent, croaking the anesthetic sting
Of loneliness. Shall he compose
    the obligatory abjuring,
Greville's Fare-thee-well to desiring,
Donne's Good-bye, sweet world,
       so soon, so abruptly?

             Waking
At dawn, drawn curtains edged with light, finding
This silken blood-purse clinging,
Body so loved, woman in all her glistening,
Begging his entrance, and more worth entering
Than the woods of Colchis, he, hot with the breath
Of essential animation, living and making,
Cannot.

      Your touch, dear sorceress.
               Damn you, is that your best?

Bleakness in the town.
                              Each house wears a grimace
Under the wind, cold and phlegmatic. Along the streets
Lie clots of old blood that are really ice.
And at Dunkin' Donuts, across
The loop of the counter, sit two young women, pristine,
Beautiful—one with her hair cropped, her face
Clear as the Cupbearer's, three rings
Of Indian silver on her fingers
That are deft with cigarettes and matches; the other
Fuller, softer, with reddening
On her nails, her hair flowing and dark. They are
So deeply in love. "Bless you, children,"
He says to the steam in his coffee. "May my weakness
Somehow still swell in your ardors a little, unbidden."
May such transmittance be?
                              Out to the bleakness.

His body, caught there in the mirror, lean
With an old man's hunger, though he turns quickly—
Not quickly enough—away. He has seen
Taut sinews, muscles thickly
Knotted with useless decades of strength, his skin
Creased and flaccid. This is an apparition
Out of an old book, an anatomy
Lesson, he *cannot* be that,
He is still the young swollen tree forever
And no gnarled bough
On an old oak rotting.

                  Spirit, deliver
Him to the true knowledge of death. He knew
It was easy. Now teach him arduousness,
How it comes slowly, how gradually, and how
An old oak declines, twig by twig, in the forest.

Your dream:
          His name was Hitler and he lived over
The yelping forest where wolves run bearing the bones
Of Tristan back and forth forever.
In a castle, in firelit rooms,
His shadow passes, enigma of the gothic tower
Become the home of horror. See there, a sword
Hopping on a hare's foot, or a disembodied
Arm that floats stiff in a bloodied
Sleeve, or maybe a boot slopping with hot liquid
That you know is not what it seems;
And there, that undeflatable phallus disguised in a hood
With one hole for the hangman's eye. Screams
You cannot hear issue from mouths you cannot mistake
In each stone of the walls. So you make your dreams
Of Hitler, you also screaming, knowing you cannot wake.

"They tossed my baby like a cat in the air
And caught him on a lance-tip, and he slid back,
Entrails popping, face gone black. 'Here,'
I gasped, bending my neck,
'Here, now here!' flinging apart my hair,
Gesturing for the blade; but they only sneered
And threw me down in the dirt and forced me,
Seven of them, with the murdering all around me,
Stench and blood and shrieking. Then they left me,
I don't know why. I begged
For the sword.
         Now more than a year after
I have this pale-eyed, wolf-pelted, thick-legged
Child. Revenge! Yet, o Ormuzd, when I get out
My knife I still see my other one, still pegged
On the lance shaft, and I cannot.
         Why! Why can I not?"

Your dream:
          Her name was Hestia, sister of God
And goddess of the hearth, a brown woman and ageless,
But known to be very, very old
And very silent. She blessed
Any house that had become a home, and so guarded
Its sanctity, yet she could dwell in the dark
Cinders as well as the glowing, and she
Was silent. Somehow this made her free
In spite of her duties. She could be felt in an instant
If the house went wrong,
If love there were not voluntary, or if wanting
Drove away giving. Silence was her song.
It meant freedom in loving. Princess, you would invoke
Hestia for your dream, but she gave you a long
Cold silent look. And, princess, you almost woke.

Why is the face in the water a woman? Because
Rita made it? Because she said it? But it could
Be a man, indistinct there, that gaze
Across eternity. Would
Other women see a man in the water, a case
Of anima/animus? No, they all always
Know that the water-person is a woman,
Just as the poem knows, the poem
Which is both. Then is it convention, the cultural
Input: Naiad, Ophelia?
Partly perhaps. But more it's a question of structural
Consciousness. For the image is basal,
From before the beginning of all imagining,
The *a priori* of human feeling, ineffaceable
For good or for ill,
      and as such it is,   it must be,   feminine.

Making love in the cabin, not to himself
This time, a visitor has come to him, has come
With him. Then, lying there, he recalls
That for a long (eternal?) moment
His being and hers were indistinguishable,
So intermingled that he could not tell
Which was man, which woman. Is that
What Plato meant by the reunited
Soul? Or his own sex-whelmed mind defecting?
Neither hypothesis
Appeals to him. He knows his feminine aspect,
Always his, deeply and dearly his.
He wonders: necessarily so are we all
And why is it hidden? Without this synthesis
How could we be, alone or together, whole?

It was Catlett driving, de Paris blowing strong,
And James P., the incomparable—he could play
Anything. But that day all along
Had been Ben Webster's, as he made that old song
Leap out of itself in greatness, never to belong
To anyone else. Oh, far and wide
The spit sprayed out on either side
Of his number seven reed to create that breathy
Tone, those growls, those flutters,
Which are all most people hear in their deafness;
But it was music, music. What matters
Was oneness, the abstract made personal in a tone.
You in your transcending freedom, never another's
Ever again,
    Ben Webster, after you've gone.

He thinks of classical women:
                                    Helen, Julia,
Thaïs, Amarintha . . .
                                    Amarintha? He smiles,
In disdain, in love. It was mythopoeia,
The convention that beguiles
Itself and its successors in a pure euphoria
Of idealization. Julia had no wart? Or
Cynthia no straggling yellow tooth?
Then they were mere conceptions, youth
Feminized, sexual but eternal, held
In the long access of rhyme
That you, dear dreamer, are inventing,
                                    romance unwilled
And unrelenting.

                    And yet that time,
He thinks, was actual; they lived, unknown women,
Flawed and misnamed, their soft rank bodies prime
For idealization. Convention is also human.

79

Near Addison now.
                    See that place over there
With the busted gable?
                    Yes, Amos.
                              Terrible,
Ain't it? All tumbledown. That's where
Dorothy lives, old Doll.
I knowed her once. By the sweet Jesus she were
The prettiest thing you ever seen. I courted her,
Courted her crazy, hot like I was—
Me and a parcel of other hornies—
But Doll couldn't never settle. Or she wouldn't.
Screwed whatever come around,
Thirteen kids and not one father amongst them,
Not as would take her off the town.
She'd be screwing yet if she could. Maybe she does,
Though I hear she hefts to nigh two-fifty pound.
Mostly she hooks rugs. You know that kind they call
    "The Blowing Rose"?

80

Your dream:
　　　　　Its name apparently is Honeywell,
But what is it? A tree of thorns, a bush, a vine
Tangled with many others, a wall
Encircling you, entwined
Twig to twig, thorn to thorn, like fire?
　　　　　　　　　　　　　　　Hell
Hath such fires, burning and consuming, themselves
Never consumed.
　　　　　　Out of the circle
Come voices corporate and low:
　　　　　　　　　　　"Oh darling,
Thank you, thank you, we are eternally yours. Only
Stay as you are and we'll burn,
We'll consume forever, and we promise there'll be hotels
On Boardwalk and Park, and champagne, furs,
Weekends in Spain, anything you want,
　　　　　　　　　　　　　　you won't be forsaken,
But we'll love and protect you as long as the world is ours,
As long as we burn, as long as you never waken."

In France, through archways, the archaic stonework
So adorned by time, he wandered the Basse-Ardèche—
Labeaume, Burzet, Roche-Colombe, Balazuc,
Towns lichened in ancientness,
Their crumbled châteaux, walls that a *trobador* took
With a song, blood-dark still where the Languedoc
Shed fierce heretical love. He wandered.
Beauty is pain plus time. Why then
Does he stay so cold? It's true, he could be at home,
And he thought of his own north,
Frozen roads, patchwork villages. He knew
The differences, naturally—colors, textures of earth,
Viticulture against dairying—and also the similarities,
Les pauvres de tous côtés et le désespoir,
He knew all right; but his heart was a cavity

Voided by too many hopes betrayed, too many
Failures. All is irrelation. What power
Could make unity? Has love any
Left in its broken tower?
What draws these themes together? Not ceremony,
That lost vantage; not belief. "The universe has only
The unity possessed by any heap."
Fact! A good fact, good to keep
(His William James) in the pocket of his mind
For a talisman. At least
It's a kind of unity, this heap, this undesigned
Collection—snow-laden spruce
And sunburnt ilex. Then there's another. Alone,
Always alone, he knew the body of loneliness,
Stone, universal stone, and the face in the stone.

La colline du mystère. Solitary here. The stone,
The old crown, is exposed, fissured, worn
By time's aimlessness, the wind and rain;
Crumbled; inscrutable; strewn;
Pieces porous and bleached, thousands, like bone.
Here on the height, alone, stands the great dolmen,
Three slabs set upright and another,
The table, a massive stone, laid over.
Une présence absolue. Inexorable, majestic,
There! And what made those
Shadowy absences, those drifted generations, wrest
And drag and raise such stones? Who knows—
Except that it was belief. It is always belief.
And forgotten. Lost. The dolmen is silent. It glows
Almost, thunderous almost in its sanctity of grief.

No love without hurt? No lovesong without distortion?
Maybe the dolmen-makers, whose art was their dinner,
Cutlets on the cave wall, and whose fashion
Of coupling was no doubt similar,
Knew more about it than we do and were right to lavish
Their loving on the dead. Is love from the grave,
Love's imagery raked from that nostalgia,
That bitterness?
                    Think of the Sangraal
And the unicorn, dear sleeper, your dream's burden,
Essential love and death.
Your couch, brocaded like veined stone, might be the
        dolmen.
But another way must come, princess,
We must love humanly, no debasement. We must sing
Our passion, as ineluctable as breath,
Without distortion, yet still this wondrous thing.

Then here was where it began, dear sleeping princess,
This stony land with its stony great *châteaux*,
Your dream's origin and focus,
The sweet song that somehow rose
As from the stone itself, *rime claire et douce*,
To sing old *jòi, valor, mesura*—oh, loveliness
Beyond all preconceiving. This,
This land of *òc*, is where your kiss
Awaits you . . .

        land of blood, of class, of hunger.
For here a song could nearly
Make nature from the world's pain, sex from anger,
A woman from death.
        But knowingly, drearily
Now we hear—so far, so near—the *trobador*
Sing, *Oc, Dieu d'amor*—wistfully, wearily—
Quora me donas jòi, quora m'en ven dolor.

Your dream:

His name was Harlequin. He wore the mask
That hides identity, which in one sense made him false,
Or in another universal, and yes, you longed to ask;
Yet you only waltz'd and waltz'd,
Tango'd, lindy'd, hustl'd, sipped from his flask
And fled with him down dim cellarways

as down the years

to the farthest, darkest cask—
Ah, was it Venice, Vienna? No matter,
Dresden will do as well. The clatter
Of years falling, decades, was like music. *O carnevale!*
Granted, his aspect was inhuman,
But why not? Who better than he who was holy
(Or might be) could keep you, dreaming woman,
Safe in your mythical cities?

And if in his mask you glimpsed

his eyes

And were saddened,

that also seemed expected,

a part of the common

Ceremony,

like a grief-rite or the children's promised surprise.

He decided to live. Alone. One room. Quaking.
Word by word he forced his poems on his rigid
Tongue. Outside, the universe smirked,
Massive, mindless, the official
Existence taunting him, haunting him, seeking
To brush him away, crush him, annihilate him, make
A no-person. And inside, meanwhile,
Simpering oblivion smiled
From every darkness, corner of room or of mind,
Beckoning as if
She could redeem, merely by her own kind
Of kindness, a murdering touch or a kiss,
His sick penis. Should he acquiesce? Very often
His longing, his simple undifferentiated wistfulness,
Almost convinced him. Yet he was anarchist, lover,

And he stood at his window and shook his fist at a cloud.
It didn't help much. It helped a little. Denial
Became, he saw, the one defense allowed
In this one-room, one-person trial
That went on for years. Well, he prayed to Ungod,
Loved, and declined to be insane. He stood
At his window for hours, by night and by noon,
Watching the bellylaughing moon,
The derisive trees, the mocking street, the cars
Singing their death-joy, the students
Walking from school and already fading, pears
Tainted on the tree. Terrified, he went
Over his terrified lines, *no* by *no*. If one shred
Of consciousness remained, one infinitesimal root
Of freedom, he swore he would save it. And he did.

The springtime so impetuous. Already pink blossoms
Are drifting down, a flurry in the peach grove
At the high end of the *vallon*. Sometimes
They become less pink than mauve,
Less mauve than deep rose, when clouds hide the sunshine
And the mountains darken. Then again they are gossamer
Weaving in brightness, falling, billowing,
Wavering. The old brown woman below
At her goat-tending looks up to see them and to see
The mysterious wind spun
From mountain stone that takes them, whirls them free
And up, up, in a vortex. With them
Her eyes too move upward. For always there is a falling
And a rising within, this beautiful helical rhythm,
And always, it seems, a vision calling and calling.

90

"My mother did it. She had to, she said. She took
Ten yards of binding cloth and wrapped my toes
Backward underneath like a broken book.
Then came the embroidered shoes,
Smaller and smaller for two years, and so I forsook
My childhood, which was my only life. Now look—
You see a Chinese lady, sixteen,
Stylish and sexy and properly constrained
For her bridegroom, who has never seen my feet
And never will, just my pretty
Three-inch shoes. Inside are pain and heat
Perpetual. They never stop. Well, I totter
In this garden, snipping carnations. Is there another
System, do you think, where girls run and a daughter
Smiles? You smile. Yes, in a year I will be a mother."

91

Came in upon him once how he might find
A freedom neither in woman nor in art.
Faith, he thought. Is it always blind?
Then the Saltmaker's part
In India he took, and of his chosen kind
At home the Dreamer's, walking through Georgia. Mind
Gave him to see them clearly, not
Ideas alone but anguish caught
In their living brains, a rational belief;
From which he saw as well
(For him afresh) how madness or any life
Lived in devotion is therefore whole,
Self-committed and therefore free, nor less
For its passivity what one could call
Powerful still in mankind's saintliness.

92

Your dream:
> His name was Heathcliff, and he was clearly
The invention of a subsidiary dreamer,
Yet how? Was he gross a little, obscurely
Not of the true demeanor,
Overdrawn? What fault was there? You loved him fairly
And could no less, since no one could say he really
Had broken the pattern. It is confusing.
His eyes are a deep darkness, losing
The pure reflection of yourself you cherished,
Which makes you love more intensely,
Suspecting your true intensity has perished.
This dream is awkward.
> Lovely princess,
Rose, are you weary now? Do you merely laugh
At all these dreaming dreams, you who are thinking
How your own great dream has departed from itself?

Your dream:
            At first its name is Heliopolis,
Beyond the Land of Goshen, where ruins have spread
Since before anyone's memory, city
Of the red sun, blasted,
Hyssop and mandrake growing in jagged fissures
And scarabs clicking in the heat. It is the center
Of known earth, ruined for all
History; it is the mouth of hell
Where hot light pours down and vanishes. So
In your dream you change its name
To Hiroshima, the city where stone-edges glow
And shadows burn in the unimaginable time
Of half-life, city of the man-made sun. Your breath
Burns in your throat. This is the most extreme
Moment of dreaming. You sleep and are close to death.

The poem moves.
                After the fierce intention,
The exalting, reaching and thrusting through lust,
Through densities of image, to explode transcendence
From a broken language, to touch
Everyone's wordlessness, to crush what was meant
Till it dances clear of language like forestfire bent
And flaring in the wind—

                Snow dances
Like fire sometimes, windblown.
                  Jesus,
Watch it! They're off the road.
                  The pickup whines
And skids in a flying drift
Of snow, wild night in the headlights. Someone
Helpless there, tentatively lifting
Her hands—down jacket, platinum hair, suede pants.
Back up then, turn, hook on the chain, shift
To low range, second gear, ease the clutch—wince

As the broken front differential pops and jumps—
But out she slips, the Mercedes with Connecticut plates,
Dragging packed snow. At once
One face goes flat,
A mask now, and a thin-gloved hand plunges,
Comes out with a twenty, an offering, a vengeance,
Insisting, commanding.
                        The wind screams.
                                        Unhook
The chain, belly-down in snow. Then:
                                Look,
Lady . . .
        Look, it ain't fitten. This is nothing
We do for the money. Take
It somewhere else.
                    And the twenty flutters,
Gasping like a fish.

                        Amos, what makes them think
They can buy us?
                    They done it—stone by stone,
Tree by tree, running brook by brook.
Hell, you and me is just something else to own.

It's awful, Amos.
                        Well, of course you could say
It starts mostly with a kind of loving. They wouldn't
Come here if they didn't like it. Why,
You and me our own selves
Don't hardly see it; don't hardly see the sky,
Nor those hills or woods or pastures. We got our eye
Always looking down in a milk pail
Or a sap bucket or up the hole
Of one goddamn animal or another to see
What ails her. We been here
Too long, wearing our butts down. But those city
People, downcountry millionaires,
They see, you bet your ass they see, our farms,
Our hills and fields, all those shapes and colors
Always changing; well, by the sweet Jesus it warms

Our own hearts too like, seems's-zo, whenever
We stop to look—it's only the best goddamn place
In the world. And them, those billionaires—
Couldn't tell a trace
From a bellyband, but they can see what's here
All laid out for them, see it some ways clearer
Than us, damn their hides, so they "falls
In love with it"—you know their flashy
Way of talking. And what do those trillionaires do
When they fall in love with something,
Almost anything? They buy it, that's what. So
Maybe it ain't just right to blame them.
They wants it and they got the power to get it,
So they gets it. You and me might do the same.
Only then the poor bastards come to feeling guilty,

Maybe because they're so damn frigging rich,
Or maybe for shoving some farmer off his land
Or the townfolk out of their housen, them which
Has come down hand to hand
For generations. So they get in a twitch
All proud and feisty-like, and it makes them itch
To buy more, and buy and buy and buy
Till they own most everything. That's why
They think they own the people too, and by God
They do, at least a good cross
Section of us. Hell, you stick a big enough wad
Of that green stuff under the nose
Of a Vermonter and he'll grab. You bet he'll grab,
Same as anyone else. And yet—
                              some of us
Won't. A few. Our own kind of pride, or crabbiness,

Or independence, call it what you blame well like.
There's some as might just call it a kind of loving,
But the other kind, the kind that makes
You give and go on giving,
Just like that, and if you get something back
You're grateful, but you don't ever ask, you don't ever
  take,
You don't ever own. That's the difference.
Some of us knows it, or senses it,
Us old north country uglies that can love a barn
Or a cow or a woman. You build
Fences to keep the animals out of the corn,
Not for a property line. A field
Is a speck of creation, just like—

                                 Ho, back down,
Amos. You're preaching now. Men here have killed
For a half-acre, and many a time. You know it.

                                          No one

100

Better, goddamn it. Why, whenever I see folks
I growed up with get so narrow-like I want
To resign, all those would-be bankers
Fighting over a misdrawn
Deed, which ain't the whole of it neither. Just think
How many of these so-called developers, these speculators,
Was home-raised country boys. We ain't
No better than we should be. But there wan't
No surveyors till the rich folk came. Them old deeds
Was drawn for a convenience
Mostly, and some of us knowed it. Likely we be
Gone now. But by God, a field is
A speck of creation, same as you or me,
So how can you own it? Tilling it is the yield.
You get because you give
                              if the giving's free.

Some don't get much, Amos.
                    Some, hell! Most
Is what you mean. Look at all these boneyards around
     here
Cram-full of them that give up the ghost
From nothing but despair,
You can damn near hear them sighing. They lost, lost
Till they couldn't lose no more, and they wouldn't cost
The state for welfare. So they lay down,
Took sick, and died—that's how it's done.
Simple. What I was talking about is not
A program, like those extension guys
With their technology; it's a feeling or a thought
Or both maybe, I don't know. Some ways
It don't work so good, like nature herself, like
A hen partridge setting six weeks on a clutch of eggs
Ain't even fertile. But look there now.
                              The truck

Slows. A bent figure in the dark, thickly clothed,
An ash staff in one mitten, flashlight in the other,
Slow-stepping from house to barn.

                                                Something's
Making that guy a bother
On a stormy night. A calving, likely. What's it worth?
Salt, coffee, a pack or two of Day's Work,
And not a hell of a sight more,
That's what he gets. Just one damn chore
After another. And yet look, that henhouse out beyond,
The woodshed and the shop,
The snowy scarecrow where the garden is, that pond
On the lower side, and over the slope
I bet you'll find an orchard keeping warm.
That light is a woman making coffee, up
And ready, case she's needed out to the barn,

Which ain't much barn at that, maybe eighteen head.
Yet they're Jerseys—can't you almost tell?—
Or even Ayrshires, sorrel red
And sweet and trained to the bell,
None of those ugly stupid Holsteins bred
With udders so big they can't hardly walk. It's dead,
Some say, all gone, finished, sunk.
Ten years sober or four years drunk
Is what I'd give this farmer. But what he gets
Is what he's got, a place,
Not just a farm but a place: sunrises and sunsets
And no damn zillionaires. And then a space
In the boneyard. Gone. Goddamn it, I feel old—
Not because I am, but the land is going, the base.
Ah, it ain't but ten below, but God it's cold.

104

Your dream is Hamlet again:
                    Is not he
Recurrent in all these appearances, the one
Prince of the North who took from sea
And solitude and stone
The thought that someone somewhere might be free?
In pain now he looks down, thinking "for me,"
Down to Ophelia in her weedy stream

Where you gaze back. You know your dream
Is his sanity and his insanity. You know
He cannot see your tears,
The endless colorless weeping into the flow
Of time, nor can he read your fears
Concerning the inevitability of act five
When you cry *love!* and no dead actor hears,

O princess,
              drowned in dreaming, asleep, alive.

105

In the mind's house of heaven the great night never
Ends.
      All the brothers are there: Berigan, Bechet,
Russell, Hawkins, Dickenson, Hodges,
And Mary Lou and Lady Day
And so many others.
               And oh they play, they
    jam forever,
Shades of strange souls nevertheless caught together
In eternity and the blues.
           No need
To cut anyone any more, no fatigue
From the straights out front or the repetitive changes,
But only expressiveness,   warmth,
Each invention a purity, new without strangeness
In that session.
           Always they strained on earth
For this thing, skin and soul to merge, to disappear
In howling sound.
           God, but it would be worth
Dying, if it could be done,
    to be there with them and to hear,   to *hear*.

Nine, he thinks, and every one a failure.
Is it accident only, the actual number,
The same as the primeval female
Faces, the nine in one?
What does that mean? And how can freedom prevail
When every lover's gift is a day in hell?
Is this finally what the face in the water
Is saying, that everyone is caught
In the terrible twist at the pit of consciousness? One
Never escapes, never.
And the sweet anarchist dream of love is gone?
What can he do, culprit forever,
But remove himself, destroy his insanity? And the mill
Of the species, grinding new culprits, new lovers,
What can it do but vanish?
                              Well, he thinks, it will.

Your dream:
        His name was unheard of, very strange,
As he himself, moving in your mind's shadows,
Gliding there in perpetual change
Like a shape on starlit meadows
In a far deserted land, was a kind of outrage
And a very deep disturbance, a danger
You had not known. He whispered, "Lady,
Will you see me, see my body
Altering in starlight, one and one and one?"
And you shuddered. Why
Was this important? What had this outrage done
To you, your world, your dream? A cry
Of anger stirred you, and then a cry of fright,
And then a broken, wistful, subsiding sigh.
You knew. You whispered back, "Hermaphrodite."

Your dream:
        Its peculiar name is Hydrogen Bomb,
Meaningless and menacing like the Minotaur
To which young couples once had come
Through their labyrinthine hour
Of passionate initiation, as to the calm
Pitiless unknown of fate. The horn of the ram
Sounds once, twice at the awful door
Of innermost darkness, and more
Cannot be said, cannot be dreamt, for this
Is the ultra-future to which
No experience leads. It is the abyss.
All is vague. Yet was not each
Dream always precisely made for this power
At the heart of darkness, this violence, this beast
Of non-existence hulking beyond your horror?

He thinks in wonder how love was all that was
At the beginning/
          The little human creature
In its blood-cave knew nothing else,
But only love, its nurture,
Its garment, its pulsing name, its pain and ease,
Its world. Then came/

            the emerging, the cold. Cause
Separated at once from effect,
A thing to be observed. Act
Was all/
       and love like dropped mercury scattered
In its parts, wandering, mirroring,
Called by such names as fear, greed, altruism, hatred,
The shattered self. World was a sorrowing,
Many voices, always cold . . ./

           Oh, take them then,
These strangely precious fragments, involve them,
    thou spirit-bearing
Word,
      in their old oneness,
           that they may be love again.

He was a soldier, he was a madman, he was a hermit,
Always in deprivation, always in love.
The cast-out seraph within him yearns
For the unattainable, to give,
To give and give: to the wounded, imprisoned, poor,
And ever to women, the captive people. What for?
He asked and asked. No death delayed,
Not one lover was left undismayed
In her ego torture. Love solves nothing. He matured
In despondency, the old deep
Melancholia. But again what for?
                              The abhorred
Stars in their slow explosion creep
Through the sky, mindless, and the mindless moon
Is a loveliness that mocks him.
                              Mind is sleep,
Dream, evolutionary error,
                    bound for extinction soon.

111

He used to think his escape was in lucidity
And refusal and rebellion. But against *that?*
To see now is to see futility.
The stars creep. What
Is human "authenticity" then but a nullity
Striving to create a value and getting beauty
Instead, dripping with blood. Will
Is the will to exploit. But still,
In his depression deepening toward paralysis,
He has one more task.
Driven in blindness, driven as the stars in their orbits,
Knowing the outcome will be grotesque,
A pain beyond bearing, and with nothing left to prove,
He must go to the princess. With nothing left to ask,
He must go,
        the prince who is human, driven, and filled with love.

Any fire will do—you who are sleeping
In "a nest of flames," Dornröschen, Brunnhilde,
In the red, red thorns, in petals fleeting—
Any burning city . . .

A fire-storm occurs when the degrees of heat
Reach 1100 Fahrenheit. Flame spreads in sheets,
A huge wind rises, soon the oxygen
Is exhausted.
   Three attacks: Mosquitoes,
Lancasters, Fortresses, with long-ranging Mustangs
To strafe the crowds.
     Next day
A leopard from the zoo sprawled in a plane tree
With two naked women below
In the charred boughs. Everywhere soldiers tried
To cremate heaped bodies with flame-throwers. Now
The smell thickens, ashes still fall, Dresden has died.

People burned, came apart, suffocated, melted.
They drowned in the Elbe trying to flee the flames.
The Zwinger was rubbled, the gardens, the Altstadt
Everywhere crazed, that porcelain
City,
    "Florence of the North,"
                      stone which exulted
For beauty, flesh for romance, all split, all spilt.

Death,
       you can be kind. You kiss
Lovers in their blissfulness. Is this
Your doing?
             Where little flames still flicker
Like rings of thorn, a crazy
Man in a smoldering coat, bloody, blistered,
Wanders and mumbles, utterly crazy,
Poking the darkness, the ashes, stumbling, rebuking
The corpses of children, crazy, crazy, crazy,
Wandering, crying, laughing, cursing, looking.

In wavering shadow and silted with soot, her face
Seems as if almost dreaming, as if under water,
Where she lies in one more ruined place
In this history of the Slaughter
Of the Innocents. How beautiful. The disgrace
Of love's civility riven like the lace
From her own breast, of death and pain
And lamentation and blood, the stain
Contaminating all the bright world she has made
Seem not to touch her.
He gazes down at her, insane, afraid,
For this will be the end. Never
Will our world lie again in her dream's keeping.
He bends to her, the real and loving other.
She wakes,
          sees,
               screams.
                    She begins her weeping.

115

Destinies, destinations: In Morrisville
Where the snow, grimed with salt-slush, is roof-high,
Two fat women, maybe nineteen
Or twenty, issue sidewise
From Tomlinson's Deli, eating without smiles
Something from the sacks clutched to their snowmobile
Jackets. Their breath is steam. They climb
Into an object of rust, which has five
Kids in the back with a black and white shepherd dog,
And one sack passes rearward.
Then this thing in its thingness, this '67 Pontiac
Station wagon, farts. Black gore
Sags from its underside. Roaring with anger,
It spins and slews, and they wobble away, gone—
One wonders where.
                    Why up over the Ben Franklin

Store, more'n likely, in one of those tenements.
Notice them childern? They'll eat the mice
Out of the mousetraps when that there candy
Gives out, of course unless
Their old man poaches them a half of venison
And sneaks it up some morning about 4:00 A.M.

Above Eden Mills a barn flattened,
Splayed and shattered under the weight
Of snow.
          It were a good-looking hip-roof barn,
Long and narrow, when I passed
This way last summer.
                         It's another farm
Gone—snow four feet deep around the house,
"For Sale" on a porch column with the agent's name
In big letters:
          FRANCIS COLE.
                         Good man, Francis.
Hates what's been happening round here, same

117

As you or I, but at least he fights hard to get
A right price for the victims. They trust old
Francis.

      Then in Lowell, the woodland cut
Over and over until all
That's left are thousands of red maple suckers and bent
Gray birches crowding a little trailer with a huge tent
Of snow covering one side.
An old woman trudges with an armload
Of softwood slabs toward the door with its garland
Of Christmas bulbs, a naked
Festoon. But the woods are gone.

                      And the Opera
In Derby Line is gone. The theater,
Gone. The music, gone.
                Where? Where?

                       Maybe

Where I'm going.
          You?
          Me. You yourself said it,
I'm nowhere. Right?
          Amos, you're in history.

Hah! Not what's wrote down, I reckon. I'm leaving
Now.
> Leaving? You don't want to see the end?
>> *I seen it*

Already, and besides I ain't even
Got enough Yankee meanness
Left for talking about what's happened. And grieving—
What's the use of it? I'll get off here. You needn't
Stop. So long. I'll see you later.

So long, Amos.
> Later?
>> Stay here,

Amos, for God's sake! DON'T GO NOW!

>> Nowhere.

And you, all of you,
Are you gone? Where is the richness of the manure
That used to steam on the snow? Some chemical
Rots the air. Are you gone? Is the land given
Forever to these mechanical monsters risen from hell?
Look at them, the clones, smiling like Richard Nixon.

119

Spirit
        whatever you are   wherever
                                Amos
Who is nowhere has been one of your emissaries
And a better than many, whence may his loss
Be told among the stories
Of the mythic people, like all those others, those
Who have lived for you, the insane prince, the inconsolable
Princess now at last in their song
Of injured bodies touching, tongue
To tongue, sorrow to sorrow, lust to lust,
A surmounting, a broken flower
In the ashes of their burnt garden, or in the dust
Of history, and then all who in their hour
Have spoken for you here, the brief attendance
Of voices and dreams.
                        Spirit
                                whatever
                        now in your own power
Speak,
        as the poem rises toward you in your resplendence.

The border is what creates illegal aliens,
Dividing what one knows from what one knows,
This called an "imaginary line,"
Not even drawn on the snow,
With a huge officious multilingual sign,
A gendarme holding its papers in its hand.
Yet there's a noticeable change. Of tone,
Of texture or feeling? One knows one has gone
As into a mirror that contains an ever so slightly
Distorted image,
Or perhaps from dreamt objectivity to the forthrightly
Seen—subjective, brilliant, undamaged.

The poem moves alone now, but without loneliness.
Self has been left among the objects that fashioned it.
Action and knowledge are one, free, far in the depths
        of consciousness.

Plains of snow. The buntings whirl like rung
Cathedral bells in the stained-glass sunlight. Crows
Flop blackly with their black song
Away from the roadkills.
Barbed wire droops. In Asbestos a song is sung
On the juke box of old men dead and of the young
Who cough and sigh: "Help us get out
Of here. We die and nobody
Cares. Nobody even knows." In Drummondville:
"You Anglais, eh? Alors
Par' la joual ici maint'non, o.k.? C'la
Ou rien, *rrriennnn!*" At Trois Rivières
The thin iron bridge crossing the St. Lawrence,
Another lordly river, clogged now, great tiers
Of rhomboidal ice-blocks thrown up on the banks,

And in the town, in neon-blaring twilight,
The disco already throbs. Northward the poem
Moves, faster now, a flight
Unaware of time
In the flow of creation, short day and long night
Mingling, past *la cité*, into the hills bright
With the glorious instincts of the wolves,
Dark with the forest's deepness, all selves
Of history risen now in one true person, past
The great white silent *lac*
Where stars fade in the aurora, and at last
Out onto the open north, ecstatic,
Beyond earth and history, the nets of essence,
Free, alone with every thing, the aurora flashing,
Trumpets, the beat of the universe, immense, immense,

And there in the sky is the known face half-hidden
In rippling lights, askance, the eternal other
Toward whom the poem yearns, maiden
Of the water-lights, brother
Of the snow-fields, Androgyne! the forbidden
Ancient of ancients granting that the poem gladden
In its free consciousness which burns
With the whole selflessness of loving, its forms
Risen profoundly from remembered voices, its tones
Heard from the great silences,
While the aurora ripples and flashes, while the snow
Gleams with its own reflected innerness
Of brilliance, brilliance, to the horizon, far
Beyond the final extremities of distance
In the beating universe,
                  the poem alone and free . . .

Princess, the poem is born and you have woken,
A world's undone.
            And it is no easy thing,
With brave romance and conquest broken,
Still to love and sing;
The tapestry is unthreaded, lovesong's unspoken
Horror spills out.
            Yet you in yourself betoken
Love's amending, for you are Rose Marie,
Pure in transcendent being, free
From history, though the Dornröschen is keeping
Your beauty for us forever.
            The sun
Will rise on the snowy firs and set on the sleeping
Lavender mountain as always, and no one
Will possess or command or defile you where you belong,
Here in the authentic world.
            The work is done.
My name is Hayden and I have made this song.

1972–1980
    Crow's Mark, Yaddo, Temple,
    Lagorce, Virginia City, Syracuse, Hamilton

NOTES

Section 1. The epigraph from Goethe's poem "Vanitas! Vanitatum Vanitas!" is difficult to translate, owing to the multiplexity of meaning in the German *Sache*. One possible translation: "I have made my concern [interest, intention, awareness, or by extension personality, self] out of nothing." See also Max Stirner, *The Ego and His Own*.

Section 3. Rose Marie Dorn was born in 1932 in Parchwitz, Silesia, a region then nominally German but ceded to Poland after World War II. Because their family name was Dorn, her parents named her intentionally after the story of *Dornröschen*, and from this felicity the poem sprang. But nothing beyond this in the poem need be construed as a personal reference.

Section 12. The "coincidental voices" mentioned earlier are placed within quotation marks. They are invented; they were heard in the susurrus of history. One hopes that the general time, place, and predicament of each speaker will be evident in what she says.

Section 15. Some readers may feel that this and other sections about jazz are an intrusion or even a mystification. Nevertheless their place in the whole poem is an important element in the complex of meanings. Readers should note, however, that the fragments quoted from songs were set down as remembered at the time of writing and are sometimes incorrect. The case for leaving them uncorrected has something to do with the essential meaning and structure of the work.

Section 21. "Brother Estlin": e. e. cummings. Reference is to a review, "America's Younger Poets," *Perspectives USA*, no. 12 (Summer 1955), p. 134. Cummings died in 1962.

Section 25. Until the advent of western science, many people of India believed that the male's reservoir of semen, located in the head, was limited absolutely, and that each discharge brought him nearer to impotence and death.

Section 27. *Per una selva oscura:* through a dark wood. From the opening lines of the *Divine Comedy*.

141

Section 28. *Perchè mi scerpi.* Canto XIII, 35, the "Inferno." Translated in the opening sentence of the section, as from the Temple edition. No further specific reference to the substance of Dante's poem is necessarily intended.

Section 32. *Lo buon maestro.* Dante's tribute to Virgil, his guide through the first part of the *Divine Comedy.*

Section 38. "Garding": *-ing* was a common folk substitution for *-en* and *-ain* during the eighteenth century and later in both England and America. Thus "Capting" in *Tristram Shandy.* Still heard in the mountains of Vermont.

Section 52. "Young Woman's Blues," Bessie Smith and her Blue Boys (Joe Smith, Buster Bailey, Fletcher Henderson). Original issue: Columbia, 14179-D, 26 Oct. 1926.

Section 59. *Zoön politikon:* the political animal. V. Aristotle.

Section 77. Sidney Catlett, Sidney de Paris, James P. Johnson. Others present, in addition to Ben Webster, were Vic Dickenson, Arthur Shirley, and John Simmons. Remarkable artists and brothers. Blue Note, no. 953.

Section 81. *Languedoc:* the name of the language, the people, and the country. Pronounced trisyllabically. V. "Lo lenga d'òc," *Working Papers,* Athens, Ga., 1982.

Section 85. "L'amour 'provençal' n'a point disparu sans laisser des traces profondes dans tous les domaines pénétrés de sa doctrine. Il a créé la politesse occidentale, la galanterie masculine; il a suscité indirectement la préciosité du XVIIe siècle.... Dans la mesure où il était chevaleresque, héroïque et maître de ses élans, il a inspiré le code galant de la noblesse française jusqu'au *Cid.* Dans la mesure où il était magique et mystique, il a créé l'amour-passion. Dans la mesure où il était aspiration à la Pureté, il a préparé la poésie italienne du XIIIe siècle, et, par Dante et le 'Dolce stil nuovo,' il influence encore la poésie moderne. Dans la mesure enfin où *il est confiance en la Nature et en l'Homme,* il demeure le seul principe sur quoi puisse se fonder une *mystique positiviste* (Auguste Comte en a repris à peu près toutes les données) et une morale de cóeur." *Les troubadours,* R. Nelli and R. Lavaud, cited in *Troubadours Aujourd'hui,* L. Cordes, Arles, 1975, pp. 19–20.

In other words everything detestable, dreary, dangerous: the modern world, outcome of *trobar* and *amor.* It is the most appalling paradox in history. Many similar statements of it have been made, of course, from De Rougemont's *Love in the Western World* onward.

142

The quotation in the final lines may be translated roughly: "Alas, god of love, who has given me so much joy, who has brought me so much grief from it." It is the conventional lament of the *trobadors*, but meaning almost infinitely more to us than it could have meant to them. In this case the line is from a *romanza* by Rambaud de Vaqueiràs (d. 1207).

Section 105. Bunny Berigan, Sidney Bechet, Pee Wee Russell, Coleman Hawkins, Vic Dickenson, Johnny Hodges, Mary Lou Williams, Billie Holiday.

Section 112. "A nest of flames": *sommeil dans un nid de flammes*. Rimbaud, "Nuit de l'Enfer," *Une Saison en Enfer*.

Section 117. The Opera in Derby Line has in fact now been restored.